"I Thought I Invented Pants"

A Hilarious Collection of 420 Moments, Plus Space for You to Add Your Own!

What's This Book About?

You know when you get super high, and you think you have the answer to everything in the universe?

This may or may not be true, but what you do have is a completely different perspective, and sometimes the stuff you come up with is actually really clever and funny.

The problem, of course, is that you're probably not going to remember any of these amazing insights unless you write them down, and if you're already high, how are you going to remember to do that?

That's where this book comes in. Keep it around for when you (or someone you know) have your moments of complete genius.

"When you are in a restaurant, and you are waiting for the waiter... you have become the waiter..."

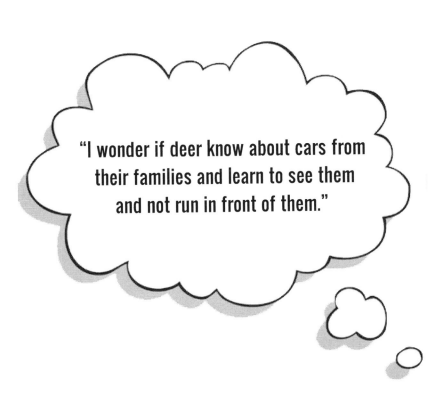

"Water is so weird.

How did humans figure out
they needed water to
survive?

Like… how did
they know what "thirsty"
was?

Also… who figured out that
water tastes better cold?"

"Hot Pockets look like
flat penises!

You cannot put a
motorcycle
in your pocket!

I want to dive into a pool
of applesauce!"

"Whoa… How do the wafers in Kit Kats stay crunchy even after they put the chocolate on them?"

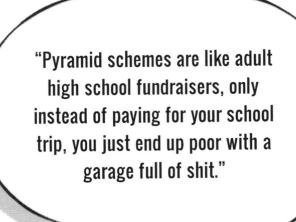

"When someone posts a picture and puts "no caption" or "presented without caption," that is actually really stupid, because saying 'no caption' is a caption."

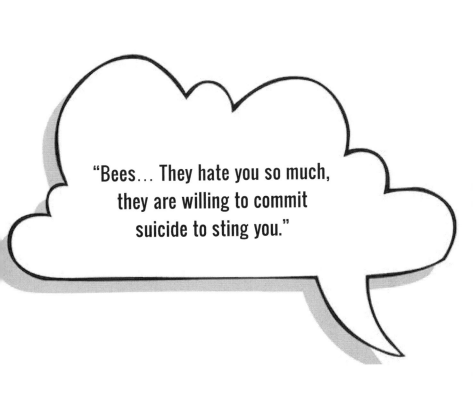

"Am I the only who finds it weird that we transfer data from one person's brain to each other's brains by opening our mouths and pushing air with vibrations into their ears?"

"Isn't it so weird that you have a little voice in your head when you're reading something…..like when you're reading this?"

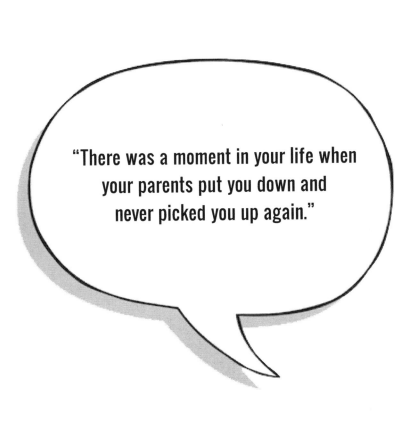

"What if people with anxiety
are just unfamiliar with
how the world works
because this is the first time their
soul has ever been here, and non-
anxious people
have been reincarnated
multiple times, so they know how
everything works?"

My parents inherited my
grandparents'
bed that was at least 50 years old,
then they gave that bed to me.

That means I am sleeping
the bed that my
parents probably conceived me in
and that my grandparents
conceived my dad in...

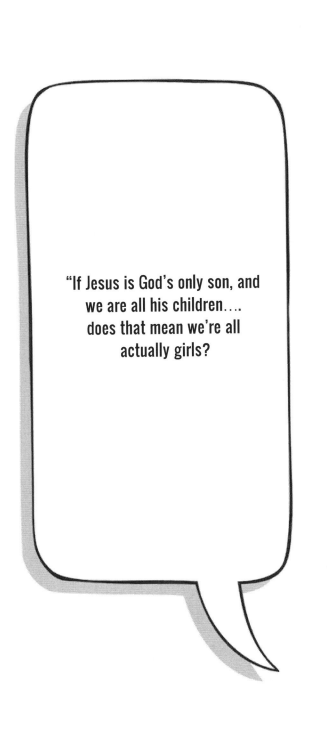

"When poison expires, does it become more poisonous or less poisonous?"

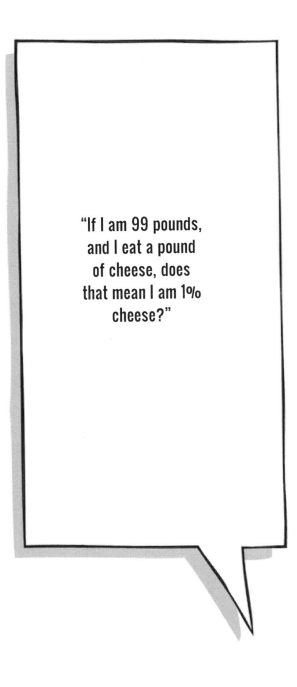

"It would be so cool if you could just live like a regular person in like, every decade in history.

But then, it would be so confusing, because just when you figured out how everything worked, you would have to start over."

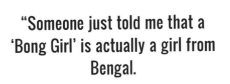

"Someone just told me that a
'Bong Girl' is actually a girl from
Bengal.

I've been using that term wrong."

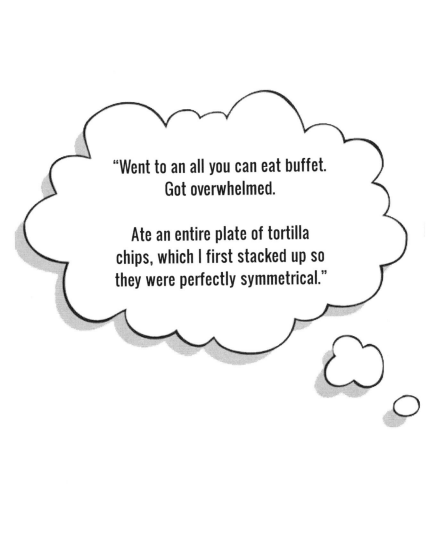

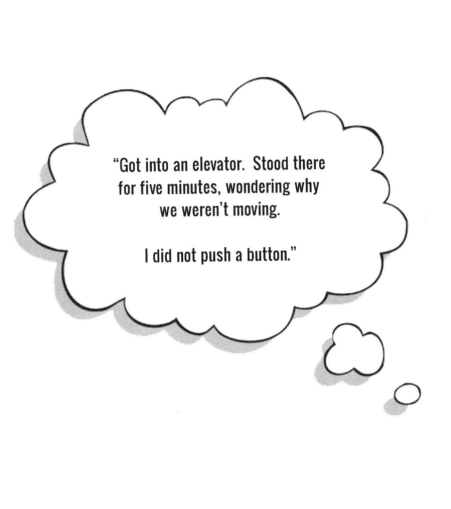

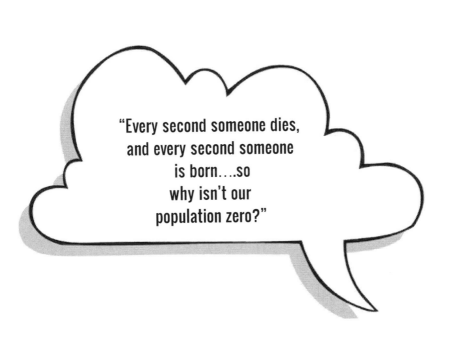

Now, Add Your Own!

You've probably already thought of some of your best 420 moments, and here is where you can write those down, so you can laugh at them later!

Almost everyone you know has done one of these (or something similar), and this is where you can start your own hilarious collection. Here are a couple of ways you might want to do that:

- Get this book out the next time you're with a group of friends or at a family gathering, read a few, and then let people start talking. Write down what they say!

- Start a post on your social media, asking people to share their funniest moments. You'll be pleasantly surprised!

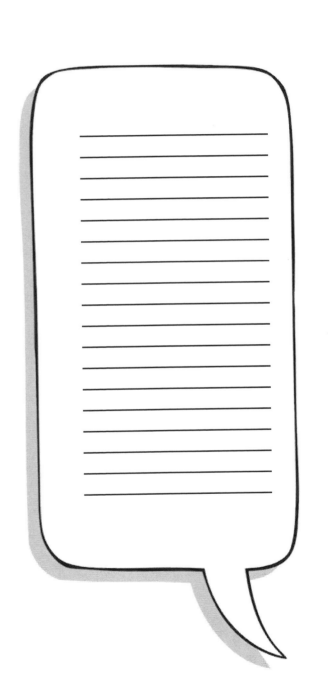

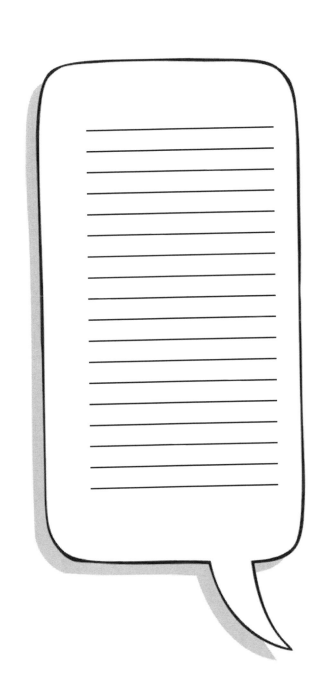

Made in the USA
Middletown, DE
06 December 2020